The Secrets of
EARTH

by Emma Carlson Berne

CAPSTONE PRESS
a capstone imprint

Capstone Press
1710 Roe Crest Drive, North Mankato, Minnesota 56003
www.capstonepub.com

Library of Congress Cataloging-in-Publication Data
Berne, Emma Carlson, author.
 The secrets of Earth / by Emma Carlson Berne.
    pages cm. — (Smithsonian. Planets)
 Summary: "Discusses Earth as a part of the solar system, including ancient astronomers' research that changed the way Earth was understood, explorations outside of Earth's atmosphere, and the possibility of sending humans to other planets"—Provided by publisher.
  Audience: Ages 8-10
  Audience: Grades 2 to 4
  Includes index.
  ISBN 978-1-4914-5863-1 (library binding)
  ISBN 978-1-4914-5896-9 (paperback)
  ISBN 978-1-4914-5907-2 (eBook PDF)
 1. Earth (Planet)—Juvenile literature. I. Title.
  QB631.4.B47 2016
  525—dc23   2014046194

Editorial Credits
Elizabeth R. Johnson, editor; Tracy Davies McCabe and Kazuko Collins, designers; Wanda Winch, media researcher; Tori Abraham, production specialist

Our very special thanks to Andrew K. Johnston, Geographer, Center for Earth and Planetary Studies, National Air and Space Museum, Smithsonian Institution, for his curatorial review. Capstone would also like to thank Kealy Gordon, Smithsonian Institution Product Development Manager, and the following at Smithsonian Enterprises: Ellen Nanney, Licensing Manager; Brigid Ferraro, Director of Licensing; Carol LeBlanc, Senior Vice President, Consumer & Education Products; Chris Liedel, President.

Photo Credits
Almay Stock Photo: GL Archive, 11; Black Cat Studios: Ron Miller, 19; Capstone: 6; Library of Congress: Prints and Photographs Division, 14 left, 14 right; Lunar and Planetary Institute: 5 bottom; NASA: cover, back cover, 1, 21 bottom, 22, Climate.nasa.gov, 26, JPL, 24, JPL-Caltech, 27 top, Marshall Space Flight Center, 27 bottom; National Air and Space Museum: Smithsonian Institution, 25; Science Source: Hincks, 21 top; Shutterstock: Daniel Prudek, 8, Designua, 9, Ismagilov, 28, Lightspring, 4, Muskoka Stock Photos, 7, photoplotnikov, 17, Quaoar, 20, 23, Steve Mann, 29, Triff, design element, cover background; Special Collections, University of Amsterdam: 13, 15; Wikipedia: El Comandante, 10, Hans Bernhard (Schnobby), 11

Direct Quotations
Page 27 from NASA Solar System Exploration profile, solarsystem.nasa.gov/people/

Table of Contents

The Secret of Life

From space, Earth looks like a beautiful marble, swirled with blue and white. But under those bright white clouds, Earth holds the most beautiful secret of all—the formula for life. And not just life, but *all* life we have found in the solar system.

Earth has the right mix of elements and available energy for plants and animals to live and grow. Earth also has oceans, lakes, and rivers of liquid water. The combination of liquid water, a protective atmosphere, and the right amount of warmth from the Sun makes Earth a place where we can live. Without those ingredients, Earth might be a bare rock like Mercury, or a gaseous, toxic greenhouse like Venus.

The earliest certain signs of life found on Earth evolved at least 2.7 billion years ago.

Fast Facts

Distance from Sun: 92,960,000 miles
(150 million kilometers)

Diameter: 7,918 miles
(12,743 km)

Moons: 1

Rings: 0

Length of day: 24 hours

Length of year: 365 days

Earth

Secret Shelter

Earth's atmosphere

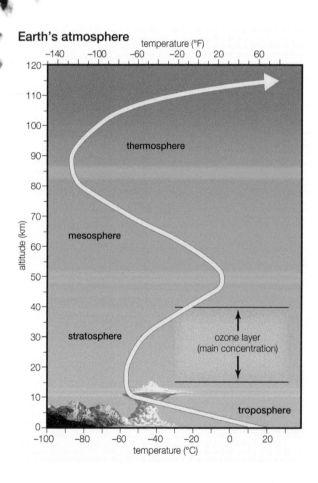

temperature (°F)

thermosphere

mesosphere

stratosphere

ozone layer
(main concentration)

troposphere

altitude (km)

temperature (°C)

Our atmosphere is our protective shelter. Without the layers of gases that wrap around Earth, life could not exist.

The atmosphere is the air we breathe. It also contains water vapor, which helps to keep the temperatures on the planet not too hot and not too cold. Our atmosphere protects Earth from meteoroids that often speed toward the planet from space. Most meteoroids burn up in the atmosphere before reaching Earth's surface.

The atmosphere has five distinct layers. The lowest is called the troposphere—this is the layer that makes most of our weather. The highest is called the exosphere—this layer merges with space.

Our atmosphere is a mixture of nitrogen, oxygen, and small amounts of argon, methane, and carbon dioxide.

Meteor shower

What's the difference?

Meteoroid = a small rock in space

Meteor = a meteoroid entering Earth's atmosphere; it forms a streak of light sometimes called a "shooting star"

Meteorite = a piece of a meteoroid that did not completely burn up in the atmosphere and made it to the ground

Forming the Earth

Earth's landscape is a mix of mountains, volcanoes, plains, deserts, and valleys. Its rolling, bumpy surface is constantly changing.

Earth's surface is made up of giant sliding sections of rock, called tectonic plates. These plates are always moving very slowly. When they crash into each other, the edges crumple, forming mountain ranges over millions of years.

The tallest mountain on Earth, Mount Everest, was created 55 million years ago. Two tectonic plates collided, and the crumpled earth became the Himalayan mountain range. Today the plates are still moving. Mount Everest still grows taller.

Sometimes magma from inside Earth pushes tectonic plates apart. Giant trenches on the ocean floor widen, and new oceanic mountains and volcanoes rise up from under Earth's surface. On land, huge rift valleys form when plates pull apart.

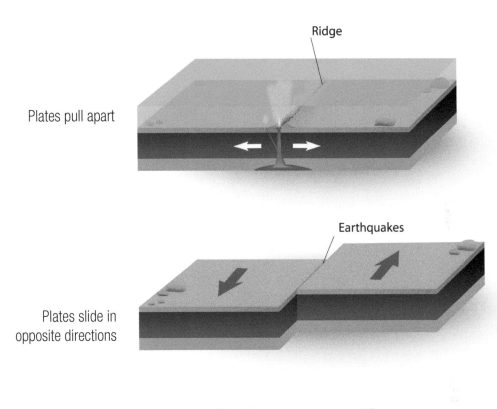

Ridge

Plates pull apart

Earthquakes

Plates slide in opposite directions

Plates collide

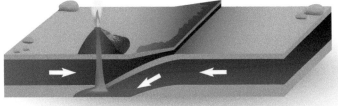

The ocean is Earth's largest habitat. 70 percent of our planet is covered with water.

Living on Earth, Charting the Skies

Ancient people watched the day and night skies carefully. They understood that the objects in the skies moved in a pattern.

The Egyptians, Mayans, Babylonians, and many other cultures were astronomers. They made charts and calendars that predicted the movements of the Sun, Moon, and stars. They also recorded lunar and solar eclipses and the lengths of years, months, and days.

Some of the earliest records of astronomical movements were written by the Akkadians. They lived in what is now Iraq around 4,300 years ago.

French Astronomer Charles Messier wrote a list of celestial objects, including star clusters and nebulae, in the 1760s. It is called the Messier Catalog and is still used by today's scientists.

Sun Around the Earth

By about 300 BC, the Greek astronomer Aristotle theorized that the Earth stood still. He believed that the planets, stars, and Sun revolved around us. You couldn't *feel* the Earth moving, he reasoned. And there wasn't wind from the Earth's movement blowing past you. Besides, he further reasoned, how would the birds and clouds keep up if the Earth were moving?

Aristotle's theory was called the geocentric model of astronomy, and it was widely supported. Almost 500 years later, Greco-Roman philosopher Ptolemy supported and advanced Aristotle's work. The geocentric model, with Earth at the center of the universe, would stand for 1,800 years.

The Greeks knew the Earth was a sphere. Before 200 BC one scholar named Eratosthenes used geometry to estimate Earth's diameter. His measurement was off by only 40 miles (64 km).

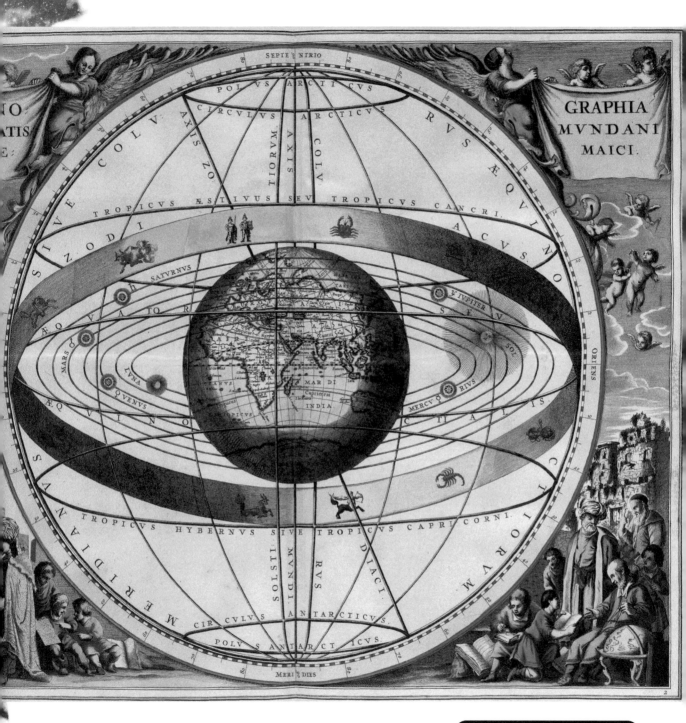

illustration of geocentric model

Earth Around the Sun

Nicolaus Copernicus was the first modern person to say that the *Sun* was the center of the universe, and that the Earth, and all the planets, revolved around it. Copernicus died very soon after publishing his theory in 1543. This heliocentric model of astronomy was very disturbing to some people. When astronomer Galileo supported Copernicus' ideas, he was imprisoned for his beliefs.

Copernicus published his heliocentric theory in a book called *Concerning the Revolutions of Celestial Spheres*.

Copernicus

Galileo

Why was the heliocentric model so offensive? The Catholic Church—which was extremely powerful—believed in the geocentric model at the time. In those years people were not allowed to publicly disagree with the Church, but Galileo did just that. For his crime he spent years under house arrest.

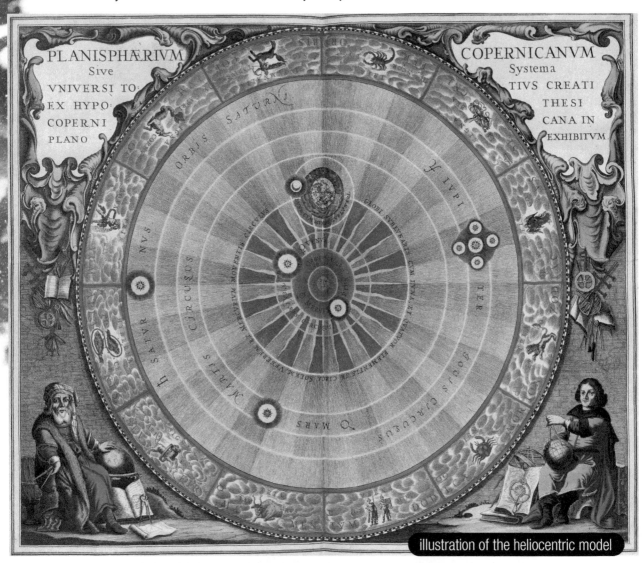

illustration of the heliocentric model

Galileo was able to build a stronger telescope than other astronomers. With this telescope he studied the planets and their moons closely. The movement of the planets and moons confirmed theories of the heliocentric model.

Journey into the Earth

In the last century people have walked on the Moon. In the future we might send explorers to Mars. We've sent spacecraft to every planet in the solar system. But we've barely explored below the surface of our own planet.

Earth is made of three main layers: the crust, the mantle, and the core. We live on the topmost layer, the crust. Below the crust lies the mantle. It is a 1,802-mile- (2,900-km-) thick layer of rock. The mantle surrounds the molten iron-nickel core.

Scientists have a plan to drill 3.7 miles (5.9 km) under the bottom of the sea, through Earth's crust, to reach the mantle. They'll remove the first fresh samples of the mantle. These samples might help scientists solve the secrets about how Earth formed and evolved.

The scientists have chosen to drill in a spot where Earth's crust is quite thin. The crust ranges anywhere from about 3 to 5 miles (5 to 8 km) thick on the ocean floor to as thick as 25 miles (40 km) under the continents.

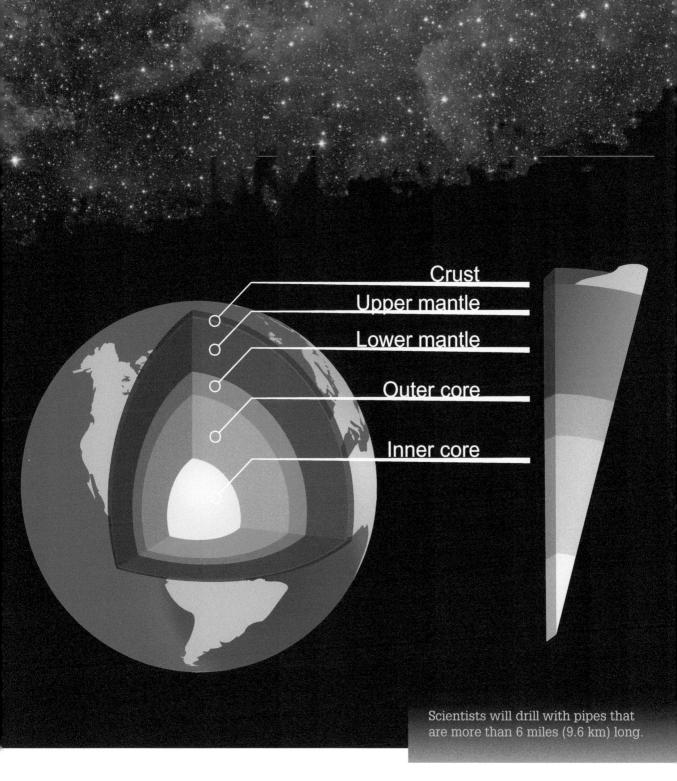

Crust

Upper mantle

Lower mantle

Outer core

Inner core

Scientists will drill with pipes that are more than 6 miles (9.6 km) long.

Our Trip Around the Sun

The weather might seem extreme on Earth sometimes. We can have freezing snowstorms in the winter. We can have blistering heat in the summer. Temperatures can range over a hundred degrees in the course of a year. But compared to the other planets in our solar system, Earth's temperature is quite stable.

Our planet rotates around its axis. The axis always points the same way in space as Earth orbits the Sun. This means that different parts of Earth's surface are tilted toward the Sun at different times of the year. This changes the amount and angle of sunlight hitting the surface, causing winter and summer seasons.

Despite the changing seasons, the shape of Earth's orbit helps to keep our temperatures fairly consistent during the year. The secret is the almost perfectly circular shape. Earth stays about the same distance from the Sun all year. If our orbit were more oval-shaped, like Mercury's, our seasonal changes would be much more extreme.

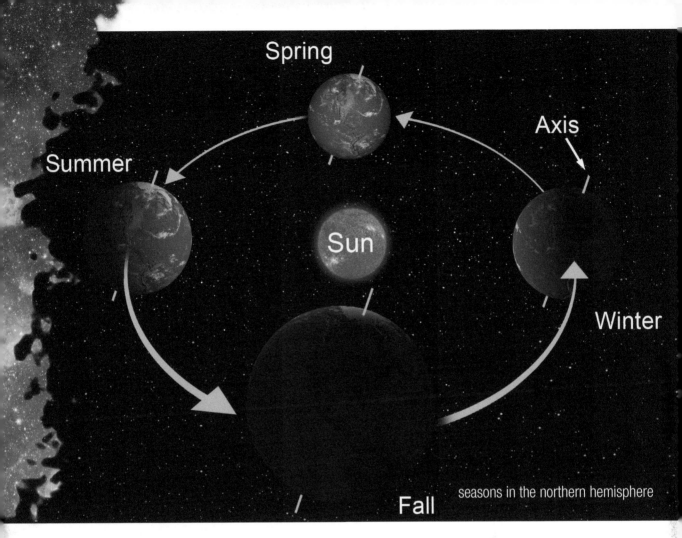

seasons in the northern hemisphere

How long is a year in our solar system?

PLANET	Distance from Sun	Length of a Year
Mercury	36 million miles (58 million km)	88 days
Earth	93 million miles (150 million km)	365 days
Neptune	2.8 billion miles (4.5 billion km)	60,190 days / 165 Earth years

Our Moon

Over the years scientists on Earth have discovered many secrets about the Moon. We know that the surface of the moon has many pools of hardened lava. They are leftover from ancient volcanic eruptions. The surface of the Moon is covered with a material called regolith—a powdery soil scattered with different types of rocks.

Scientists think that the Moon was created soon after the solar system formed. A small planet may have slammed into Earth. Hot material from the surfaces of both planets shot into space. This material stuck together, eventually forming the Moon we know today. This idea is called the Giant Impactor Theory.

Sea of Tranquility

The average distance between the Moon and Earth is 238,855 miles (384,400 km).

illustration of the Giant Impactor Theory

The First Man on the Moon

Astronaut Neil Armstrong will always be remembered as the first human to set foot on the Moon. Wearing a spacesuit, Armstrong stepped out of the Lunar Module onto the Moon. His words were broadcast live around the world. "That's one small step for a man, one giant leap for mankind."

Mission: Apollo 11

Landing Date: July 20, 1969

Landing location: Sea of Tranquility

Crew: Neil Armstrong, Buzz Aldrin, Michael Collins

The Moon and the Earth

The tide's coming in! You've probably heard that before. But did you know that it is the Moon causing the oceans to rise and fall?

Earth's gravity pulls on the Moon, keeping it from flying out into space. But the Moon has its own gravity too. The Moon's gravitational force pulls on Earth and its water, causing the tides to shift.

The Moon affects Earth in other ways too. Earth has a natural wobble as it spins. The Moon's gravity helps to steady it. This helps to keep Earth's climate steady.

Astronauts who walked on the Moon would often fall—there is barely enough gravity for their bodies to sense up from down.

Twelve people have walked on the Moon.

The Moon's gravity is much weaker than Earth's. A person who weighs 100 pounds (45 kilograms) on Earth would weigh only 16 pounds (7 kg) on the Moon!

23

Mission: Orbit Earth

Before Neil Armstrong set foot on the Moon, humans were already exploring Earth's orbit and atmosphere. The Soviet Union launched the very first artificial satellite ever to orbit Earth in 1957. It was called Sputnik.

The United States launched its own satellite in 1958. It was called Explorer 1 and it sent back information about radiation in space. A race for space exploration began. Within five years the Soviet Union and the United States sent astronauts into orbit around Earth.

EXPLORER 1
AMERICA'S FIRST EARTH SATELLITE

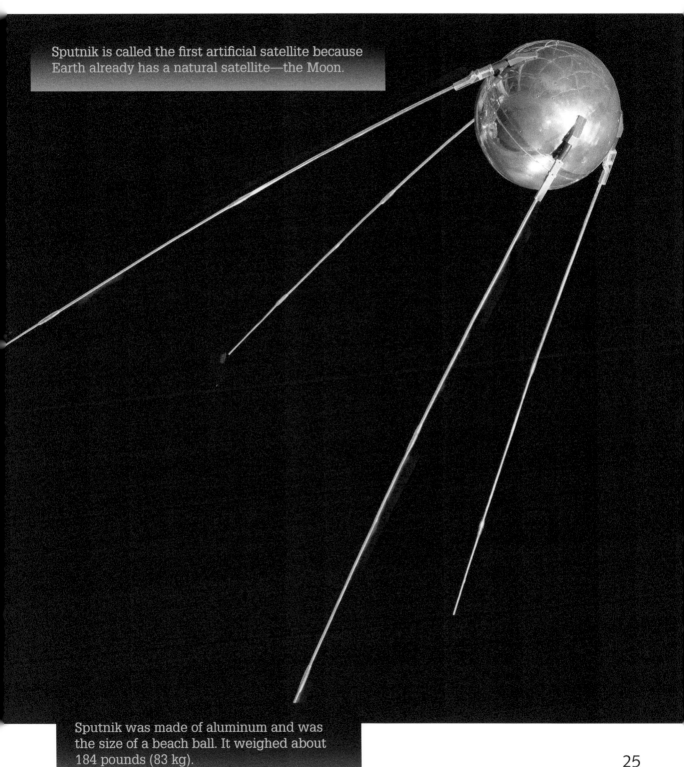

Sputnik is called the first artificial satellite because Earth already has a natural satellite—the Moon.

Sputnik was made of aluminum and was the size of a beach ball. It weighed about 184 pounds (83 kg).

Satellites and Space Science

More than 2,000 satellites currently orbit Earth. They watch our weather, measure changes in forest cover, and inform navigation systems. They help us make phone calls, give us television signals, and spy on enemies. A satellite completed a map showing 99 percent of Earth's topography in 2009. Another satellite was launched in 2011 to measure how salty the oceans are—and it's taking these measurements *from space*.

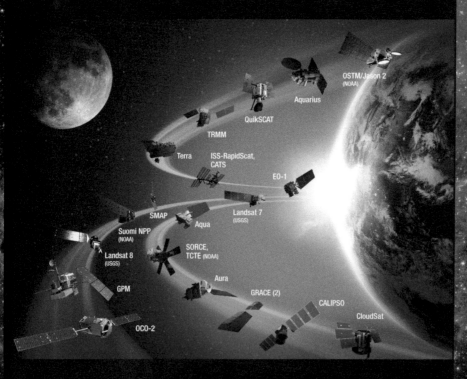

Jason-3 satellite studies oceans

Scientist Spotlight: Mark Boudreaux

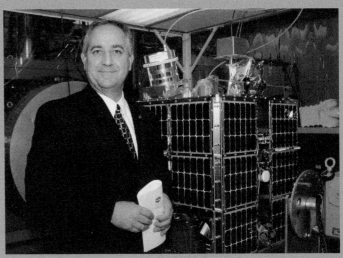

Mark Boudreaux remembers bringing a black-and-white television set to his school in Thibodaux, Louisiana. It was the 1960s and he wanted his class to watch the Apollo rockets blast off. Fifty years later, he's one of the scientists who helps launch spacecraft—namely the FASTSAT (Fast, Affordable, Science and Technology Satellite). The FASTSAT looks at Earth and does research on Earthly things, as opposed to looking out into space. When asked about the most exciting moment in his career, Mark said, "I was in a state of awe the first time I climbed aboard a space shuttle to perform a flight instrument test. I remember pinching myself and thinking: 'How did a small town guy like me get himself into this incredible situation?'"

Flying into Space—Briefly

Until very recently space travel was almost always funded by governments. But in the not-too-distant future, many more people might be able to travel into space. Super-fast, super-powerful airplanes could take us high into Earth's atmosphere. Passengers would be able to experience the feeling of weightlessness for a few moments. They would be able to look out the window and see the Earth floating below. Some say it's one of the greatest sights in all of humanity.

There is so much to learn about our solar system and our place in it. Even though we live here, Earth still has lots of secrets to uncover.

The company Virgin Galactic wants to take people into space. Their suborbital spaceship is made of two aircraft. The "mother" ship carries the passenger ship up to the edge of space, then releases it.

Virgin Galactic passenger ship

Private citizens who want to pay $35 million can actually travel to the International Space Station onboard a Russian spaceship.

Glossary

astronomy (uh-STRAH-nuh-mee)—the study of stars, planets, and space

axis (AK-siss)—an imaginary line through the middle of an object, around which that object spins

diameter (dye-AM-uh-tur)—a straight line through the center of a circle, from one side to another

element (EL-uh-muhnt)—in chemistry, an element is a substance that cannot be split into a simpler substance

evolve (ee-VOLV)—to change or develop slowly, often into a better or more advanced state

gravity (GRAV-uh-tee)—the force that pulls things down or to the center of a planet and keeps them from floating away into space

magma (MAG-muh)—melted rock found beneath the Earth's surface; magma becomes lava when it reaches the surface

molten (MOHLT-uhn)—melted by heat; lava is molten rock

orbit (OR-bit)—the invisible path followed by an object circling a planet, the Sun, etc.

radiation (RAY-dee-AY-shuhn)—energy that comes from a source in the form of waves or rays that you cannot see; can be dangerous energy

rift valley (RIFT VAL-ee)—a long valley formed by tectonic plates separating

satellite (SAT-uh-lite)—an object, natural or man-made, orbiting a planet or a moon

suborbital (suhb-OR-bit-uhl)—an object that does not quite go into orbit around Earth or other planet, but which comes close

topography (tuh-POG-ruh-fee)—the detailed description of the physical features of an area, including hills, valleys, mountains, plains, and rivers

vapor (VAY-pur)—particles of moisture in the air

Read More

Nardo, Don. *The Blue Marble: How a Photograph Revealed Earth's Fragile Beauty.* North Mankato, Minn.: Compass Point Books, 2014.

Sneideman, Joshua. *Climate Change: Discover How It Impacts Spaceship Earth.* White River Junction, Vermont: Nomad Press, 2015.

Tomecek, Steve. *Dirtmeister's Nitty Gritty Planet Earth: All About Rocks, Minerals, Fossils, Earthquakes, Volcanoes, & Even Dirt!* Washington, D.C.: National Geographic Society, 2015.

Internet Sites

FactHound offers a safe, fun way to find Internet sites related to this book. All of the sites on FactHound have been researched by our staff.

Here's all you do:

Visit *www.facthound.com*

Type in this code: 9781491458631

Check out projects, games and lots more at
www.capstonekids.com

Critical Thinking Using the Common Core

1. What are three ways Earth's atmosphere protects life on our planet? (Key Ideas and Details)

2. Read the text on page 10. Why did ancient cultures study the night sky? Do modern astronomers have the same reasons? Do they have any different reasons? (Integration of Knowledge and Ideas)

Index